March 13th Publishing
Las Vegas, Nevada USA
Copyright © 2025 *La' Kendrick Thompson*

MARCH 13TH PUBLISHING

Edited by: Penelope Stickney
Cover Photo: La' Kendrick Thompson
Cover Design: La' Kendrick Thompson
Author Photo: La' Kendrick Thompson

Authors Info:
Ldthompson81@yahoo.com

Visit the author's website at:
amazon.com/author/lakendrickthompson
ISBN: 979-8-234-00580-9

Naked

La' Kendrick Thompson

Table of Contents

Section 2: Love

Hard

Complicated

Run

Enough

Numb

Sapiosexual

Small World

Dream Girl

Perfect

War

Thirst

Unapologetically

The Spider

Unglued

Fool

Hearts

Beautiful

Cold

Souls

Demon

You

Hugs

Journeys

Flowers

Boomerang

Tug-of-war

Closure

Lost in your love

Nothing

Love in the air

Section 5: Knowledge

Faith

Father

Prayer

Warriors

Jesus

The Cross

The Light

Lost you

The Greatest

The Burning Bush

Gracious

Divine Intervention

Glory

Rebirth

Understanding God

Rejoice

Losses

Forgive me

Dedication

To my mother…
You once said I was destined for greatness, I hope I'm making you proud.

Forward

When we live our lives with honesty and engage with others through our conversations and personal views of life, we can be thought of representing our emotions as "Naked." How can we sometimes respond to life's challenges? We cannot ignore them although we may try and when we experience surprise attacks we are astounded and occasionally more aggressive in our responses. Life is not simple. Although nothing may change, understanding life situations may come easier and maintain a better response when we retreat, examine, and think through the emotion of the event. Whoever we are and in whatever situation, it's better to stand back and refrain from an illicit response. It may become a new direction, but our lives do move on.

La' Kendrick Thompson has experienced these surprise attacks on his life and has recorded them in several of his previously published books. In this book of his poetry, Thompson opens his emotional sensitivity and places himself before us. *Naked* demonstrates his honest depth to his experiences and permits us to interpret his comments into a better understanding of our life experiences. In times, we experience emotional loss or seemingly ignorant outside attacks, and within these poems, we can take his hand and listen to his wisdom. His poetry can help us regain strength in our lives.

There is part of us that believe we can fight and survive no matter what we think (or our emotions) may know. It's not so strange. Where there's still life, there's still hope. When we recognize this and refocus our lives, we realize that what happens in life is up to a living Savior. It has been a blessing to work with La' Kendrick on this book of his poetry.

Penelope Stickney

Section 1: Pain

<u>Naked</u>

I'm naked
My soul
Is bare
I'm open
My flaws
Exposed
No clothing
I'm broken
These walls
Are closing
The truth
Unloading
The lies
Disposing
This life
I'm loathing
I'm hoping
I'm praying
Dear God
I'm chosen
I'm naked
There's nothing
To hide
I'm open

Defeated

My soul is defeated
There's no sense in fighting
When every breath I take
It feels like I'm dying
There's no sense in trying
When all I do is fail
My soul is defeated
My life's a living hell
I've struggled by myself
I didn't ask for help
I hustled on my own
Took every single step
To make it out that hole
To climb from the depths
Success means nothing
When it ends in my death
My soul is defeated
The devil is a threat
My life is falling apart
I can't help but fret
There's one constant thing
The stress is repeated
I'm done trying to win
My soul is defeated

Lungs

I reminisce about the past
With tears in my eyes
My cries are from guilt
I developed over time
Moments I took for granted
I wish I could rewind
Though memories fade
The thought of you has never strayed
I prayed this pain would leave but it remains
A broken man dying inside what I became
I'll never be the same after such a tragic loss
No matter what I've gained I still feel lost
Without you in this world
I'm in a state of shock
If only I could turn back the hands on the
clock
To do something different
To change the outcome
To help you breathe again
Put air inside your lungs.

<u>Darkness</u>

Black clouds hover over futures of brightness,
Obscures your existence and marks you with
blindness.

Lifeless when darkness has paralyzed the iris.
It spreads like a virus and makes you feel
spineless.

No longer shining, the sun has dissolved,
Trials, tribulations, and storms have evolved.

The sounds of blackness are like melodies of
gloom,
It weakens my spirit to vibe to these tunes.

Minds are consumed with thoughts that are
painful,
More losses than gains, more demons than
angcls.

Darkness is more than the absence of light,
Darkness is also the absence of life.

Strength

I've been fighting since birth
Still fighting till this day
I'm tired of being strong
How much strength does it take?
I'm trying not to break
It's hard to keep it together
When trials and tribulations
Disrupt my endeavors
Every decision becomes an error in judgement
I'm afraid to choose
It's to the point I'm reluctant
I'm tired of being strong
Tired of being tenacious
All I've done is survive
I'm tired of being courageous
I've been fighting since birth
When will I get a break?
I'm tired of being strong
How much strength does it take?

<u>Lost Vegas</u>

Lost in the desert
Searching for my heart
I dropped in the sane
It's buried in the dark
Amongst the dry heat
The cacti and palms
It hasn't rained in months
My heart is made of stone
Lost in the desert
Without a sense of calm
Searching for my heart
The love in me is gone
A hundred ways to sin
It's hard to stay strong
The city has my soul
The whereabouts unknown

Loner

A house full at home
I still feel alone
At a loss for words
My mind's in the zone

A phone full of contacts
No incoming calls
Or none outgoing
I don't want to talk

Rain

As a kid I thought the rain
Could wash away the pain
But when the sun returned
All appeared the same.

The rainbows were beautiful
Multi-colored hues
The air was filled with moisture
The sky was light blue

The neighborhood I knew
Might've had a different view,
But the calm of a storm
Couldn't make it transform

All left were leaves,
And trees on the ground
The same ugly squalor
Before the black clouds.

__Zombie__

When your spirit dies
You become a living corpse
Forced to be alive in the ugliest disguise
No sense of direction as you roam back and
forth
With tears in your eyes so people are mortified
Your smile is to hide all the pain you feel inside
The bad memories that have left you
traumatized.
Trapped in a never-ending cycle of affliction
Resorting to addiction,
To make it disappear.
A temporary fix when your heart is still aching,
No matter how much alcohol and drugs you
have taken
You're mentally awake, but physically asleep
Everyone avoids you and thinks you're a creep.
Afraid your bad luck is going to rub off on
them
No one wants to call you a friend
When you're a zombie.

<u>Grief</u>

I can feel it like it just happened
The worry in my gut
The uncertainty
The very moment lightning struck
The lump in my throat
The incapacity to speak
The pain in my chest
The irregular heartbeat
The food aversion
The days that I couldn't eat
The insomnia
The nights that I couldn't sleep
The suffocation
The inability to breathe
The devastation
Praying it's just an awful dream

S.I.B. (Self-Injurious Behavior)

I cut myself to stop the bleeding.
The pain brings me pleasure.
The tension is high
Although it hurts, I feel better.
I feel a rush then the pain subsides.
For a moment it no longer hurts to be alive.
I take a deep breath and suddenly I'm relieved.
I've injured myself, so my shirts have long
sleeves.
I don't want to be judged; you couldn't grasp
the reason.
The tension is high,
I cut myself to stop the bleeding.

Naked

<u>Waiting</u>

So good things come to those who wait?
I've been waiting for a while,
How much waiting does it take?

I want to break free
Free from all the madness,
But it's impossible to flee from all the sadness

There's nowhere to run,
There's nowhere to hide
Tell me how can I escape from my own mind?

My own thoughts are my worst enemy
It's like I'm on a battlefield fighting with the
inner me.

Dear God

I don't know what's gotten into me
Whatever it is I think it's out to finish me
I'd be damned if I'll let this be the end of me
So, I must keep searching for inner peace
I wasn't raised to be weak

Naked

I have a strong mind
I'm not the type to feel defeated
I'm the strong kind

The wrong kind to quit fighting
And stop His mission
I've been waiting a long time
The clock is ticking

__Purpose__

Get over it they say
Time heals wounds
Plenty of time has passed
My heart is still bruised
My smile is not authentic
My laugh is generic
The person on the outside
Hides his true feelings
I'm crying on the inside
I'm barely hanging on
Existing in this world
But I'm already gone
I've left the stratosphere
I truly hate it here
I'm questioning my purpose
What am I doing here?

<u>Struggle</u>

It's been difficult to cope
The hope in me is dark
The future feels grim
Resentments in my heart
Embarking on this path
To forget about my past
To live in the present
Like every day's my last
Focused on the Lord
Instead of what's in store
Careful with my words
My tongue is my sword
Every day is a struggle
To feel like I belong
I'd like to live in peace
What am I doing wrong?

<u>Recovery</u>

It's a wound that never fully heals
A scar that never leaves
A constant reminder of all the good memories.
You left a mark on my heart for eternity
So, when it beats, I know that you're still here
with me
Hoping your spirit appears and it's clear to me.
Knowing you're near and dear would give me
mental peace
A conversation is needed so I don't overthink
Preferably at night so I can find sleep.
I wish I could take things back to how they
used to be.
The past is the past but it's still new to me
And I've learned there's no telling what a day
might bring.
You tell me what's worse? Nightmares or
daydreams?
Either way I'm still haunted by the same thing
And I've been in denial. It's time to come clean.
Acceptance is the first step to recovery.
Acceptance is the first step to recovery.

I Wonder

I wonder how it feels
To not have a headache
To not feel heartache
To not be in a dark place.

I bet it feels great
To not be in pain
To not feel insane
To not feel drained

I wonder how it feels
To have joy inside
To not want to cry
To not want to die

I bet it feels great
To be a happy person
To not feel uncertain
To feel like I'm deserving

Section 2: Love

She fell in love with a poet

She fell in love with a poet
His words were alluring
She'd given up on fate
His odes were assuring

A Love that's enduring
She found it in a stanza
A heart filled with questions
He had all the answers

In every single line
He wrote with precision
As if he read her mind
When no one else listened

When no one else cared
His words were heroic
A hopeless romantic
Fell in love with a poet

I can't believe it

The wind blew me here
I landed in your arms
A stiff breeze
Sent me to a land
Unknown
Foreign
A culture
I'm not accustomed to
I never heard your language
I can't converse with you
Your niceness is scary
I'm leery
It's weird
I'm used to dysfunction
The wind blew me here
There must be a motive
Why?
What's the reason?
You chose me to love
I still can't believe it

Love

Love is an open book
Filled with many pages,
A story of commitment
Respect and admiration

Love goes through stages
Filled with ups and downs,
There's peace and there's war
It's like a battleground

Love is profound
You'll know it when you have it,
It's not easy to find
So don't take it for granted

Love is problematic
You may go through a break-up
Say some hurtful things,
Then turn around and make-up

Love is great enough
To bring peace during wars

Naked

Love is so strong
It can calm any storm

Love makes you glow
Like the sun moon and stars
Love has its bumps,
Bruises and scars

Love keeps you warm,
When the world is cold
Love is forever,
Love never grows old

Love is therapeutic
It mends broken hearts
Mistakes are forgiven
We must show remorse

Love is private,
But it should be revealed
When love is a weapon
It must be concealed

Love is a dream
But it's not make believe

Naked

Love is reality
Love is everything

Mood

I'm in the mood for love
But not an ordinary love
Nothing is cliché
It's separate from the norm.
The world doesn't exist
We've created our own,
An alternate universe
No one else calls home.
We dance to a different rhythm
A different song
Bonded by a melody
A self-centered tone
A love that is rare
Not a worry, not a care
A love in which we're lost
In the moments that we share

Insomniac

I have trouble sleeping
When I think about your love.
I'm sure you are the one, but you told me we
are done.
It was fun while it lasted, you said you needed
more.
You're exploring other options and you're
walking out the door.
I implore you to consider all the promises you
made.
I believed in your words and your actions were
the same.
Maybe I'm to blame for misplacing my faith.
I put you above God, so He snatched you away.
I have trouble sleeping
My heart constantly aches
My mind constantly races with thoughts of
being replaced.
My eyes are getting heavy, and my body is
relaxed
But I can't fall asleep.
I'm an insomniac.

The Awakening

You awakened my love
When I was asleep
I was minding my business
Enjoying my peace.
You opened the door
I entered your space
I told you my fears
You said it was safe.
I told you about my past
You knew I would break
You wasted my time
You lied to my face.
You told me you've grown
You want something real
You opened more wounds
I needed to heal.
You said you were different
You're nothing like her
You said you won't hurt me
You treated me worse.
I pulled it together
Now I'm a mess
You awakened my love
And now I can't rest

<u>Relationships</u>

The writings on the wall,
We've been through it all,
I've hurt you, you've hurt me
It's nobody's fault.
I learnt that in relationships everyone walks,
Physically or mentally, we come to a halt.
When relationships are dead
They're outlined in chalk
They're taken to the morgue
Then buried in a vault.
Relationships hurt like salt inside wounds
Eventually you'll heal but it lasts many moons.

Reciprocations

If she loves me so,
I must love her back.
If she's cooking me food,
I must take out the trash.
If she's washing the dishes,
I must empty the rack.
If she's rubbing my back,
I must run her bath.
If she's washing my clothes,
I must pump her gas.
If she's mopping the floors,
I must cut the grass.
If she manages bills,
I must hand her cash.
Everything's reciprocated
Or it won't last

Trust

Thirsty to be loved, in search of a fountain,
even though my heart feels rocky like the
mountains.
The times I've been disappointed may be in the
thousands.
On my knees praying for a love that's
astounding.
Steady counting my blessings, filled with
emotions, picking up the pieces of a heart that
was broken.
Open to the notion, although it's hard to mend,
When I'm fully healed, I can love once again.

Fake love

Fake love is the norm
The real is deformed
An abnormal gesture
Often not performed

My heart is worn out
From all the high usage
Sharing my true emotions
With those who are abusive

For once in my life
I would like to feel safe
To experience the truth
Not a love that is fake

<u>Sleeves</u>

My heart is on my sleeve
You're mad when I wear it
It's written on my face
You dread my appearance
I'm careless
Speechless
Lately I've been distant
I hardly ever smile
No hugs
No kisses
It's written on my face
You can tell when I'm lying
My heart is on my sleeve
No way I can hide it

Hard

Loving you is hard
You got too many flaws
You got too many scars
You keep your guards up

You never let me in
Your past is your present
Your past was a lesson
Your past has me stressing

You're messing up the future
You lack a sense of humor
You entertain the rumors
Loving you is hard

You're very disrespectful
You always want to fight
You nag day and night
You always think you're right

You got too many rules
You got too many shoes
You got too many purses
You come with too much baggage

Naked

Your attitude is savage
You are my biggest challenge
Your heart has been damaged
Loving you is hard.

Run

I don't know what's going on
But something feels wrong
The synergy is off
The chemistry is gone.

I can feel it in my gut
The energy is strong
We don't talk much
We don't even get along.

All we do is argue
We never have fun
You make me feel awful
You make me want to run.

<u>**Numb**</u>

The pain doesn't hurt.
I can't feel a thing.
I'm immune to your touch,
It's more than skin deep.

My insides are hollow.
From what you've done to me
My heart no longer beats.
I can't feel a thing.

Naked

<u>Sapiosexuality</u>

Our minds intertwined
Intellectually connected
Our chemistry's electric
I'm mentally aroused.

Your style is poetic
What you feel you express it
You're unapologetic
I'm mentally aroused.

Our conversations epic
Our bond is magnetic
Your thoughts are my fetish
I'm mentally aroused.

You're everything I cherish
Every moment I relish
You're sex without caressing
I'm mentally aroused.

Small World

I was told it's a small world
And it's true
We were physically apart
But still heart to heart
A couple distant strangers
But closer than we thought
Although we crossed paths
We never stopped to talk
I never stopped to think
She might be the one
I might be her moon
She might be my sun
She got me seeing stars
My head's in the clouds
Another chance meeting?
The same place and time.

Dream Girl

Where have you been after all of these years?
After all of these tears, you're finally here.
You only appeared when I slept through the
night, and when I woke up you were nowhere
in sight.

For most of my life I've been taken for granted,
giving my all, but left empty handed.
A heart that was damaged, you've come to
restore.

My cup overflows, with love you have poured,
deep in soul, you truly are a blessing.
Do dreams come true?
You've answered the question.

Perfect

In a perfect world
You would be the perfect girl
I would be the perfect guy
We would have the perfect life.

We're both perfectly flawed
So maybe it was destined,
For us to be together
With all our imperfections

War

My love for you is deep
But my hate for you is deeper
There is no in between
It's either hell or heaven.
You make me feel angelic,
And wicked all together
There's truly no denying
My love for you is dying.
Our pulse is getting lower
Our heartbeat is slower
We need defibrillation
I think this life is over.
You cardiac arrest me
You make it hard to breathe
Your love is suffocating
You are my lung disease.
The sweetest on the outside,
But sour underneath.
The casualties of war
There's never any peace.

<u>Thirst</u>

I'm thirsty for love,
I need a full cup of her
She's fresh like the water I consume from the
earth.
She poured into me, helped recognize my
worth,
My thirst was quenched for a moment but now
it hurts.
She left me feeling empty,
Now my mood's dry,
Dryer than a desert,
I used to feel alive.
Essential to our lives,
I need her to survive.
I had a sense of pride when she stood by my
side.
I wasted her time,
I didn't recognize her worth.
Her cup was empty
I never poured into her.
In need of the same water, I consumed from
the earth.
She needed to feel alive.
She was dying of thirst.

<u>Unapologetically</u>

The damage is done
Wasn't a temporary fix
There's no turning back
When the act was permanent.
It can't be erased
It was done purposely
It wasn't a mistake
Not a moment of uncertainty.
Everything was thought out
Premeditated actions
Preconceived notions
Prior to what happened
Thoughts of repercussions
Disregarded logic
This is what we wanted
We didn't try to stop it.
No begging for repentance
Or asking for forgiveness
Was willfully committed
No care if there's a witness
Surcly it was wrong
The infidelity
Nevertheless,
I love you unapologetically.

The Spider

There's a part of me that loves you
A part of me that hates you
A devil on the inside
The beauty of an angel

I love to see your face
But the sight of you is painful
Entangled in a web
It's hard to escape you

Unglued

We used to stick together
Couldn't pull us apart
For better or for worse
It hurts more and more
To know I might lose
My most prized possession
Nothing monetary but the time I invested
We used to stick together
Nothing could come between us
Our bond was unbreakable
We couldn't be defeated
What happened to forever?
I thought we'd never lose
We used to stick together
We're coming unglued

Fool

A fool for love
You must think I'm stupid
Because I'm still here
After everything you've done

Loving you is difficult
I've tried to walk away,
Packed all of my bags
And handed you the keys

A fool for love
You must think I'm dense
Because I came back
After all you had said

Your tongue was a sword
You cut me with your words
Stabbed me in the heart
And never apologized

A fool for love
You must think I'm insane
Because I keep trying
To repair what is broken

Naked

This time will be different
It seemed like you changed
A bunch of false promises
To make sure I'd stay

A fool for love?
There's proof I'm a fool
When I'm in love
All do all I can do.

Hearts

The queen of confusion,
Meets King of delusion
A beautiful disaster
With an ugly conclusion
The illusion of love,
The origin's thrill
It's all a mirage
Till someone gets killed.
Perishing hearts
Filled with acrimony,
The blood becomes dry
The heart becomes stony.
The queen of temptation
Meets the king of persuasion
An amazing misfortune,
With a shaky foundation.

Beautiful

Beautiful you are,
Although you feel ugly
I know your guard's up
But I need you to trust me

Beautiful you are
Although you never hear it
I know you're less confident
From your broken spirit

Beautiful you are
Although you're teary eyed
I know you feel worthless
But you don't have to cry

Beautiful you are,
Although you feel depressed
I know you want to give up
But keep doing your best

Beautiful you are
Although he mistreats you
I know you've said your prayers
But God hasn't freed you

Naked

Beautiful you are
Although you can't see it
Your faith has been destroyed
And it's hard to believe it

But beautiful you are

Cold

The coldest winter is not as cold as your heart

A serial killer,

An assassin you are

There's ice in your veins

Your temperature's extreme

Your thoughts leave me frozen

Stiff like a breeze

Your attitude's chilling

Your words are so raw

The coldest winter is not as cold as your heart

Your tongue is so sharp

It cuts through my skin

With absolute precision

Crisp like the wind

Your company is nippy

When I see you, I shiver

Your seasons are frigid

Naked

It's always December

The coldest winter is not as cold as your heart

A serial killer

An assassin you are.

<u>Souls</u>

She inhales my love
But not inside her lungs
She welcomes all my energy
But not with open arms
She spreads her legs
To embrace every flaw
Everything I've done
In the past that was wrong
Every place I've gone
She traveled far beyond
All my past trauma
Those other women caused
The pain I've endured
She accepted every scar
And allowed me to enter
The center of her heart
Despite my imperfections
She lowered her guard
Our souls are connected
We built a close bond.

Naked

<u>Demon</u>

She's a demon in disguise
She hides behind a mask
A camouflaged lover
Masquerades as an angel

She stalks her prey
Studies each move it makes
She lies in wait
Then attacks from every angle

A poisonous creep
She's the mark of the beast
In her web of deceit
She'll have you entangled

The epitome of fire
She knows what you admire
Aware of your desires
She's willing & she's able

The master of confusion
Her beauty's an illusion
A happy home she ruins

Naked

She hates it when you're faithful

As wicked as they come
Her job's never done
A demon is one
But she has many labels.

<u>You</u>

I don't want to lose you
I still choose you
What must I say or do to prove to you?
There's nothing I wouldn't spew
Nothing I wouldn't do
To show my gratitude
That's how much I love you
You're the only one for me
I'm the only one for you
I don't know if you believe me, but every word
is true
You're the only one I see
I only have eyes for you
Your earthly protector
I'm willing to die for you
I've cried over you
Lost my mind over you
No matter what I say
I can never be over you
I vowed not to leave
I owe my life to you
I had to walk away
Didn't want to fight with you
It hurt like hell
I couldn't say bye to you

Naked

But like a boomerang
Came right back to you

Boomerang

How did I allow myself to be in this position?
Back to where I started
At the same place I left.
You've thrown me away
I was hurt I'll admit it
Despite what you've done
I returned in an instant

Hugs

She loves to be held
But not held accountable
She places a veil over all that she does
A hug says I'm sorry
There's no resolution
Everything is foggy
She causes confusion
Her weapon's affection
An intimate distraction
Blinded
She doesn't see the flaws in her actions
Her arms wrap around me
I start feeling bad
Questioning myself
Am I wrong for being mad?

<u>Journeys</u>

I saw the warning label, but I looked past the
signs
Threw caution to the wind
Wool covered my eyes.
I chose to be blind instead of a visionary
A beauty that was glaring, became my
adversary.
Staring in the window of a soul that was dark
I didn't stand a chance I was doomed from the
start
Embarked on a journey I should've traveled
alone
I couldn't bring joy to a heart made of stone.

Flowers

The mystery of you
The curiosity of me
The panoramic views
Of what's hidden underneath

Beneath all the beauty's
A heart that does not bleed
In need of CPR
To resuscitate the streams

The blood flows freely
The growth spurts have begun
Like plants that are watered
With the right amount of sun

A flower that's repaired
Cares more about the florist
Out of all the broken vines
You were picked from the forest

Tug-of-war

I've made compromises
She's made compromises
But when we disagree
We have trouble compromising
No one wants to budge
She tugs
I tug
We're both at the end of our ropes
Through with love

Closure

I know you've been depressed
I haven't done my best
To make you feel safe
So, you've made idle threats
If I don't change you may change your address
Other birds are chirping
You need a better nest
I hope you realize how blessed you truly are
Despite all your wounds you overcame your
scars
It's hard to accept but I need to let you go
We're stuck in the same position
We both need to grow
There's something I need to know
Before you spread your wings
Was it true love?
Because it was to me.

Lost in your love

I'm lost in your love
I don't know where I'm headed
We've traveled on this journey
But somehow, I am stranded
I landed in this place
That has caused further damage
I gambled with my feelings
When my heart couldn't stand it
I knew I shouldn't have chanced it
Now it's too late
I'm lost in love
My heart is misplaced
I'm searching for answers
To why it must end
I'm now left to wonder
Where is my best friend?
The person I trusted
Is gone with the wind
Never to be found
You've taken my love

Nothing

There's nothing I can do
Or nothing I can say
To change your point of view
To make you feel safe

There's nothing you could hear
Or nothing you could see
To help you understand
To make you believe

There's nothing I could buy
Nothing I could create
Nothing I could try
To put a smile on your face

There's nothing you could do
Or nothing you could say
To change my point of view
To push me away

<u>Love in the air</u>

There was love in the air
The atmosphere was calm
Her company was warm
Not a worry in the world

Our minds weren't there
Love took us elsewhere
To another sphere
We couldn't see or hear

Outside of our domain
Nothing else mattered
But the moment we shared
Our love filled the air

<u>Love Since 1981</u>

A love like this is impossible to find, our hearts are in sync, beating at the same time.

The perfect unison is impossible to teach. A natural rhythm we share the same beat.

Love since I was born, since 1981. God had you in mind. Our path was designed.

I was on cloud nine, swept off my feet. You would finish each sentence, predicted what I'd speak

A daily encore, love stuck on repeat. Long as I have you, there's no thought to cheat.

Got me thirsting for more, I need another drink. Parallel to the earth's core, our love is that deep.

Love since I was born, since 1981. God had you in mind. Our path was designed.

You're the window to my soul. When I look in your eyes, my spirit is refreshed, you make me feel alive.

My heart has been revived. With you I found life. If loving you is wrong, I don't want to be right.

I was searching for love, you were in plain sight, right up under my nose. You're the love of my life.

Naked

Love since I was born, since 1981. God had you in
mind. Our path was designed.

My mind and hearts are conjoined. I feel you in my
skin, the same DNA, like conjoined twins.

Caressing you mentally. Is this bad for my health?
You are a mirror image. I'm in love with myself.

Love since I was born, since 1981.

Fate

I believe I found paradise
In a world filled with hate
Her mere presence is heaven
I'm at the Pearly Gates
It must be fate
Her company is quite refreshing
Positive energy
It feels like a Holy blessing
She was created for me
She came from my rib
Promised to give her my all
As long as I live
God forgive me for placing her on a pedestal.
What I feel is platonic It's nothing sexual
What an incredible feeling it is to be adored
We operate on the same plane
On one accord
You adsorb my energy
You know me well
The Lord brought us together
Our love will prevail.

<u>Criminal</u>

Is it a crime?
To feel how I feel
You've played hard to get
I'm in it for the thrill

Should I be arrested?
For time I invested
To have you in my arms
The penalty is excessive

I'm guilty as charged
A criminal at large
My heart is apprehended
For life I am sentenced

<u>Blessed</u>

It's been about her
Since the first day we met
The good and the bad
I have no regrets

She was there all along
There was a date set
A moment in time
Our hearts would connect

We've been through the rain
The storms have been swept
A gift from the heavens
Lord knows I'm blessed

__Survival__

True love survives
When tried it prevails
It finds a way to win
It sustains when there's doubt
It's all about us
Everything we do is plural
Yet we became one
The day we took an oath
We vowed to be together
Till death do us part
In sickness and health
Whether rich or poor
We've been through it all
The storms came and left
We built a foundation
On rock instead of sand
Put God in the center
It's where our faith lies
Through trials and tribulations
True love survives

Separation Anxiety

I need you to be closer
You're too far away
Suddenly you're distant
I didn't ask for space

You changed in an instance
You pushed me away
There's no communication
Very little to say

The silence is enormous
You've spoken loud and clear
Without saying a word
You confirmed what I've feared

Refusing to accept it
Feeling completely stunned
The pain of rejection
Wondering what I've done

To cause you to flee
Seeking another destination
I'm not worthy?
I don't deserve an explanation.

Naked

I've come to understand
Love has an expiration
I thought you'd always be near
Can't stand the separation

Contagious

Your love is contagious
Similar to Vegas
You cater to my vices
You satisfy my cravings
It's hard for me to fight this
Feeling of excitement
The thought makes me tingle
I'm smiling as I write this
I know your capabilities
Mentally and physically
Were spiritually connected
A different type of energy
Your love of contagious
It spread like a virus
Enticing me with beauty
Pleasing to my iris

Section 3: Lust

<u>Physical Touch</u>

It stays on my mind
More often than it should
How frequent I've indulged
I'd stop it if I could
Ashamed to admit it
The fear of being judged
Or misunderstood
It feels like a drug
My way of showing love
To feel reciprocation
My language is to touch
A physical engagement
It makes me feel wanted
Craved and desired
Impossible to harness
It's just the way I'm wired

<u>Heart to Heart</u>

Thrust into action for both our satisfaction
Don't know if this is lust, we feel or if it's
passion
Imagine if our hearts could articulate the
feeling
Entry and embracement
Warmth and sensation
The feeling that we feel when we reach our
destination
A heart-to-heart talk is the deepest
conversation
Pulse rates increasing
The true meaning of love
Thrust into action our wills are imposed
The longer we connect
The more our hearts grow
Extended conversations,
Egos are being stroked
Warmth and sensation
Evoked by your presence
A heart-to-heart talk
The deepest conversation

Hot

Scalding flames

When I see you

I feel the fire

A burning desire

To feel the heat between your legs

Passion ignites

The entire mood is set

Our temperatures rise

The entire room is lit

Warm and wet

It's hell on earth when we're naked

Doused in flames

It's like our bed's fumigated.

Sweltering heat

The sweats dripping from our bodies

I don't want to cool off

I like it better when it's hot

Wet

Shower me with your love
Rain on my parade
I don't need an umbrella
Let me feel your cascade
Let me surf in your ocean
Feel your tidal wave
Remove your river dam
Open the flood gates.
Be my hurricane Katrina
I hope the levee breaks
Let me fish inside your pond
I hope you take the bait
Let me sail in your sea
Swim inside your pool
Drown inside your lake,
Drain in your lagoon.
Let me play inside your bay
Burst all your bubbles
Wade in your water,
Then lie inside your puddle.

Power

The most beautiful treasure,
A pleasure to look upon,
A value you can't appraise,
Worth more than you could fathom.
More precious than diamonds from Sierra
Leone,
A sight for sore eyes
And the greatest gift to man
Created with beauty in the eye of the beholder.
Wonderfully made,
Curvaceous and alluring.
The entire room lights up
And heads start turning,
Necks start breaking,
And mouths begin to water.
Thoughts become lustful,
Pockets become flat,
Seeds are planted,
A new life emerges.
Addiction takes over,
Marriage begins and ends
Friends become jealous
By the power of a woman.

<u>Temptation</u>

I know it's in my nature
The beast in me is crazed
The urge is addictive
It's difficult to tame
Temptations my opponent
It comes from every angle
The body of a demon
The beauty of an angel
The presence of a woman
Her presence is distracting
A challenge to ignore
When my body is reacting
The flesh becomes weakened
Energy's seductive
I'm willing to indulge
It feels self-destructive
Discipline is needed
To overcome defeat
Temptation is a trap
Resistance is the key

<u>Lipstick</u>

Smears of her lipstick
A heart-shaped image
Painted on his frame
In a red-shaded pigment.
Evidence of mischief
Kisses on the collar,
No ordinary squalor
There's a trace of dishonor.
Leaves one to ponder
If the co-defendant's new,
The lipstick suggests
That it happened out the blue.
An organic attraction
You've only dreamed about it,
A helpless reaction
No time to think about it.
Once the damage is done
It's written on his face,
Smears of her lipstick
A permanent disgrace.

<u>Chains</u>

Confused you with love
You're two different beings
One comes from God
The other comes from demons
Two different feelings
Could end in disaster
The thrill of the chase
It was love I was after
Captured by the flesh
You bound me with chains
Made me feel relieved
When love brought me pain
You made me feel close
To those who were distant
When I felt neglected
You brought me attention
Now that you're a sickness
I wish you would leave
It's time for me to heal
Love is all I need

Lust

Ever since the first time I've been chasing this high.
My body feels tense when I haven't taken a hit.
It stays on my mind more often than I'll admit.
I'm obsessed with the feeling I don't know if I should quit.
My flesh remains weak; despite the strength I've gained.
This demon has a hold on my physical frame.
I've been tamed by this beast in the form of a woman.
Her feministic qualities are absolutely stunning.
I answer when I'm summoned, I'm becoming an addict.
It's too hard to resist, it's my only bad habit.
I'm more than a fanatic, I'm completely obsessed.
When I can't sleep at night, she puts me to rest.
An indescribable feeling, it gives me a rush.
I'm forever held hostage by this thing called lust.

Section 4: Awareness

<u>Inheritance</u>

Sins of my father
I inherited his ways,
As if he'd written a will,
And left all his traits.
A gift and a curse to be versed as a charmer,
What makes it even worse, I got his bad
karma.
No life insurance policy,
No monetary gain
The only thing he left was a lifetime of pain.
Sins of my mother,
I inherited her drive,
She gave me all the tools that I needed to
survive.
I cried swimming pools of tears after she
passed.
A lifetime of pain much different than my dad.
She didn't have much, but she left me
everything
Sins of my parents on the day I was

<u>Talk</u>

If I could talk to the younger me, I'd tell him,
"Keep your head up."
Life is going to knock you down, but you better
get up

Talking to the younger me I'd tell him not to lie

Never be afraid to say what you feel inside

Talking to the younger me I'd tell him be
yourself

You don't ever have to pretend to please
someone else

Talking to the younger me I'd tell him dry your
eyes

No matter what you're going through God is on
your side

Talking to the younger me I'd tell him to be
smart

It's okay to fall in love but they're going to
break your heart

Talking to the younger me I'd tell him to be
strong

Naked

When you're weak pray that God strengthens
you to carry on

Talking to the younger me I'd tell him to
beware

You're gone lose your mother, so you need to
be prepared

Talking to the younger me I'd tell him not to
bother

You'll finally get to meet him but you're going
to lose your father

Talking to the younger me I'd tell him not to
cheat

Your marriage will be tested daily but you can't
be weak

Talking to the younger me I'd tell him, "It's
your fate."

The younger me is why the older me is doing
great

Smile

I envy your smile

But not why you'd think

It's not because of your lips

Or pearly white teeth

The twinkle in your eyes

Or the dimples in your cheeks

The sound of your voice

And the joy when you speak

I envy your smile because I wish it was me

Who could let go

Live

And have inner peace

Be the life of the party

Rejoice and be free

Not a care in the world

Just laughter and glee

Peace

My peace is everything

I refuse to be disturbed

By any negativity

To whom it may concern

My peace is everything

It can't be jeopardized

It's not up for discussion

It won' be compromised

My peace is everything

I need some good karma

It's positive vibes only

So you can save the drama

My peace is everything

I'm not interested in gossip

Naked

What he said or she said

Anyone who's toxic

My peace is everything

If your energy is off

I can't have you in my circle

I don't even want to talk

My peace is everything

I'm in a good place

I'm happy to be alive

You can see it in my face

My peace is everything

Roses

I want my bouquet while I'm here to say thanks
Don't wait until I'm deceased to tell me I was great
Don't wait until my funeral to toss them on my grave

Put my roses in my hands before it's too late

I'm not talking flowers that were purchased from a florist

Planted in a garden

Provided sun and water

I'm talking recognition

A true celebration

Hand me my roses

To show appreciation

Depression

Depression is real,
It's not a bogus diagnosis
Fabricated for sympathy,
Pretending to be hopeless.
We hide behind a smile,
So one doesn't notice,
Internally we're broken,
Refusing to be open.
The walls are closing in,
Patience is extra thin,
We're always in our heads
We're living on the edge.
Depression is real,
It makes it hard to sleep
Our minds never rest,
Because we over think.
Late nights are dark,
The days even darker
Constantly being judged,
It makes our lives harder.
Depression is real
Don't' you ever think it's fake
Trials and tribulations,
There might be a day.

Problems

I don't have solutions
All I have are problems
Confusion is at my table
A plate full of problems
I pray before consuming
The food I eat is toxic
My thoughts convoluted
I don't know how to solve it
My mind is polluted
My brain feels foggy
I don't have any answers
Yet and still, they call me
As if I have solutions
When I all I have are problems
I'm searching for a way out
This door that's revolving

<u>Wings</u>

If I had wings
I would soar like an eagle
Fly far away
With my head in the clouds
Escape all the noise
Find a quiet place
Where I can think clearly
And focus on my craft
Preferably an island
One that's deserted
A warm sunny day
With a slight summer breeze
I would land in the sand
On a blanket by the ocean
Listen to the waves
A moment of reflection

Escape

They'll miss me when I'm gone
When I'm far away from home
I'm feeling out of place
This is not where I belong
Reality's fake
I need another place to roam
Somewhere I can dream
Maybe an empty road
Where I can be alone
Never misunderstood
Somewhere I can think
Like cabin in the woods
Surrounded by a lake
To get a mental break
In the middle of nowhere
Somewhere to escape

<u>Summers</u>

The sun shined brightly
The temperature was warm
The summer breeze was light
The neighborhood was calm

The clouds turned gray
The wind started blowing
The black men armed
For the never-ending storm

<u>Storms</u>

A storm isn't forever
It has to end,
And after all the rain
The sun shines again.

Watching the downpour
Storm's last longer
But if you're not killed
It will make you stronger

Stare out the window
Pray for better days,
Trust your faith
Or the weather won't change

<u>Self-Love</u>

Searching for self-love
I've lost my identity.
The person I've become,
Seems more like an enemy.
Mentally drained,
This relationship is tiring.
Nothing makes me happy
It's an unhealthy environment.
Time is expiring
I'm running out of tries,
Living my truth,
Because I'm running out of lies.
Honestly, who am I?
I probably couldn't tell you.
Ma, I know you're watching,
I hope I haven't failed you.
Searching for self-love
I didn't have the tools
To fix a broken heart,
To change my point of view.
How do I love me?
I didn't have clue.
I lost everything,
The moment I found you.

Avow

I don't want to let you in
Not even as a friend
You remind me of a place that I've already been
A sin I've committed and begged for repentance
Memories of a time I vowed not to revisit

My Downfall

I can hear whispers
Gossip and chatter
Celebrating my losses
Cheers and laughter
Hands that are clapping
Names that I'm called
Heads that are bowed
Praying for my downfall

Experiences

One of these days
It will all make sense
The pain
The suffering
All I've experienced
All I ever heard
Will then serve a purpose
All I ever seen
Will become perfect picture

Never

Never give up
Never quit
Never stop,
Never throw in the towel
Never sit
Never squat,
Never sit on your ass
Never chill
Never relax,
Never point the finger
Never blame
Never ask,
Never cry like a bitch
Never complain
Never beg,
Never explain
Never be lame
Never scared,
Never be broke
Never lie
Never cheat,
Never fold under pressure
Never snitch
Never be weak,
Never finesse

Naked

Never hate
Never run,
Never forget
Never leach
Never be dumb,
Never say never is the saying,
Never sleep
This can go on forever
But this is never for me.

Time

Time waits for no one
It never takes a break
The clock keeps ticking
Whether sleep or awake

Time moves forward
You can't press rewind
Focus on the present
And never look behind

Time can't be wasted
Make sure you stay on track
When it's gone it's gone
And you'll never get it back

Time is valuable
It's worth every second
Every minute, every hour
Every single day is precious

Time is of the essence
It can't be delayed
When something is important
Get to it right away

Naked

Time is money
And it should never be exempt
Make sure it's understood
That you're worth every cent

Time heals wounds
It alleviates the pain
As the years pass by
But you'll never be the same

Freedom

Let the bird out the cage
Release the inner rage
Illustrate what's been eating at your core,
Liberate.

Divulge what you're feeling
Become an extrovert
All you have is your freedom
Become one with your words.

Exercise your right
The very first amendment
Verbalize your thoughts
Illuminate your wisdom

Escape the mental prison
Become a fugitive
Your enemy's restriction
Your freedom is a friend

Naked

<u>Truth</u>

The truth is horrific
No one wants to hear it
It doesn't set you free
It incarcerates the spirit.

Most people fear it
It doesn't make you brave
Admitting you were wrong
It makes you feel ashamed

Shackles on your brain
From thoughts of being judged,
Critiqued and criticized,
By everyone you love

When push comes to shove,
There's undeniable proof,
That most people lie
Because they hate the truth

<u>It's Okay</u>

It's okay to fall
As long as you rise
Stand to your feet
And hold your head high

It's okay to fail
As long as you tried
The key to success
Is to never say die

Empathy

I can feel what you feel
I've been where you've been
I'm willing to absorb all your pain from within
When your energy is off
My skin begins to crawl
I'm here to lend an ear
I'll open my heart
I'll listen to your problems
Whether big or small
I'm waiting in the shadows
To guide you when it's dark
I'll catch you when you fall
If you call, I will answer
When you're not around
I won't tolerate the slander
I'll come to your defense
Against all your enemies
With me it's all love
I'll always have empathy

Immortal

When the light turns dark
I'll soon be forgotten
There's truth in the phrase
Out of sight
Out of mind
Creatures of the moment
The memories will fade
The more time passes
The less I'll be remembered
Gone in the flesh
My presence and my aura
The only thing remaining
The truth in my poems
My psalms will never die
My cries are eternal
Death couldn't kill me
My words are immortal

<u>Man</u>

Silence is my loudest cry
Can you hear me?
Telling you I'm hurting?
My heart is torn apart.
I've been emasculated
Constantly disrespected
Internally I'm dying
It's to the point I'm speechless
No one hears me out
Or ask how I'm doing?
I'm expected to be strong
No matter what occurs
If I show them signs of weakness
They start calling me names
Like soft
To make me feel less of a man

Section 5: Knowledge

<u>Guns</u>

Shots in the dark
Shots in the broad day.
Shots in the park
Shots while the kids play.

Shots at the bar
Shots while we celebrate.
Shots at your car
Shots while we navigate.

Shots when you're talking
Shots when you're quiet.
Shots when you're honest,
Shots when you're lying.

Shots when you're walking,
Shots when you're running.
Shots when you're sober,
Shots when you're buzzing.

Shots with your hands up
Shots when you move.
Shots when polite,
Shots when you're rude.

Naked

Shots when you're innocent,
Shots when you're guilty.
Shots when your record's clean
Shots when you're filthy.

Shots from your neighbors,
Shots from your spouse.
Shots at your front door,
Shots in your house.

Shots when you're in bed
Shots when you wake.
Shots at your funeral,
Shots at your wake.

Shots at the school,
Shots while the kids learn.
Shots at your job,
Shots while you earn.

Shots when it's cold out
Shots when it's warm.
Shots when it rains,
Shots when it storms.

Shots when your skin's black!
Shots when you're white!

Naked

Shots when you're dead wrong,
Shots when you're right.

Shots when you're old,
Shots when you're young.
Shots in America
Obsessed with our guns.

__Bridges__

Bridges get burned and routes must change.
The path once crossed you may never walk
again.
Be careful with your words, you may never talk
again.
Everything you said could cost you in the end.
Appreciate the bridges that are present in your
life.
Handle them with care, make sure you treat
them right.

Versus

Black versus white
Day versus night
Death versus life
Blind versus sight

Christ versus Satan
Curse versus praying
Love versus hating
Single versus dating

Paying versus buying
Truth versus lying
Laughs versus crying
Defeat versus trying

Fighting versus peace
Strong versus weak
Woke versus sleep
Shallow versus deep

Unique versus common
Top versus bottom
Disease versus condom
Solution versus problem

Naked

Starving versus greed
Wants versus needs
Trials versus plea's
Slave versus free

Knees versus standing
Justice versus anthem
Shacks versus mansions
Ugly versus handsome

Réaction versus cause
Perfection versus flaws
Crimes versus laws
Right versus wrong

Dealers versus users
Beggars versus choosers
Targets versus shooters
Winners versus losers

Reparations

The land is cursed
I've seen blood on the leaves
Where dead bodies dangled,
Hanging from the trees.
The stench of rotten corpses
Piled in mass graves
Burned to a crisp
With no guilt or shame.
Dark forces roam the earth
Looking for racists
Humiliated men
Victims of buck breaking
Women who were raped
Babies who were taken
Sold on auction blocks
To build this wicked nation.
The land is cursed
We're in need of reparations
The ancestors earned them
It's time to make payments.

<u>Skin</u>

They used to make fun of me because I'm
dark-skinned
I didn't realize love comes from within
The brighter your skin
The better world treats you
If you're not strong
They'll certainly defeat you
Impossible to win
Being ridiculed by my friends
Throwing stones
As if my skin is a sin
When your tone is brighter
You're on a higher plane
No better than the racists
Making me feel ashamed

Ebony

Your smooth brown skin brings me joy from within.
You are the perfect hue, a reminder of my roots.
Proud to be black, even though I've had doubts.
It's worth all the hate that has spewed from their mouth.
It represents strength, symbolic of the culture.
The power to withstand all the years we have suffered.
The color gets defamed, and we are the ones to blame
But when I look at you, there is no guilt or shame.
Proud to be black when no one else cares.
I love your big lips and the texture of your hair.
I didn't mean to stare,
I was caught up in the madness.
I wanted you to know I appreciate your blackness.

Trees

We've lived different lives by the color of our
eyes.
Completely different views are based on our
hues.
Brown versus blue, this determines what we've
seen.
A nightmare compared to a peaceful night of
sleep.
The lies she's been told; she's intrigued by the
truth.
She was warned I'm a tree that only bears
bitter fruit.
Forbidden to partake she decides to indulge.
She comes to realize all the lies she was told.
My skin is a sin she refuses to repent.
In her eyes it was fate and no coincidence.
Her family disowns her as long as she's with
me
I can never be accepted on her family tree.

Negro

I can never be a hero

I'm just another Negro,

More concerned with looks,

Instead of reading books.

I'm viewed as a crook

Even though I'm educated,

A law-abiding citizen but still investigated.

I am the most hated.

I'm just another Negro,

No matter what I do they'll still treat me like a zero.

I am an entertainer, a doctor and the president, but

Just another Negro,

I'll always be a suspect.

<u>Babies</u>

Fathers making babies
Babies having babies
Mothers left alone,
Tending to her babies

Single parent homes
Babies with no guidance
Babies left alone,
While mothers are providing

Fathers are dead beats
Mothers barely surviving
Fathers run the streets,
Babies are defiant

When fathers are absentees
Babies turn to violence
Mothers are in grief.
Too many babies dying

Mothers stressed out
Mothers sick of trying
Babies acting out

Naked

While fathers are hiding

Crazy World

Mass hysteria
No one's exempt
There's some form of crazy
In all who exist
To meet the criteria
Be
Interact
Society's passengers
Drove to the max
Bipolar
Anxiety
Paranoia
Psychosis
Manic
Depression
And more
Diagnosis
The culture
It impacts
From grown-ups
To babies
Birthed into chaos
The world is so crazy

Americans

Birds of a feather,
We never flock together,
Completely segregated,
Divided by our races,
Our customs and our cultures,
Humanistic vultures,
Quick to pass judgement,
Mass media puppets.

<u>Energy</u>

Consuming negativity is bad for the spirit,
Appeasing to the ear, but destructive when
hear it.
It's sweet like a pastry, but sour like a lemon.
Once the fruit is bitten, it's a part of your
existence.
Inhaling damaged goods from broken men and
women,
Is similar to bad food destroying the liver.
It enters your mind, and your soul becomes
eroded,
Watch what you absorb, make sure it's not
corrosive.
It might seem delicious but is it really
nutritious?
Is the person infectious, a threat to your
condition?
If the answer's yes then you should keep your
distance,
Protect your energy; keep the drama out your
system.

Section 6: Guilt

<u>Who's crying now?</u>

Tears pouring from her eyes
I watched as she wept
Her soul left her body
She died a slow death
I watched as she cried
The source of her condition
I didn't give a damn
I paid her no attention
I watched as she mourned
Crumbling inside
Time healed her wounds
Her pain would subside
The roles would reverse
She watched as I wept
The source of my condition
I died a slow death
As I took my last breath
Karma's her name
The same energy was kept
She watched as I mourned
The tears of a clown
My soul left my body
Who's crying now?

Dead

I know you're still living
I know you're still breathing
You still have a pulse
Your heart is still beating
A mind of your own
I know you're still thinking
How could you forget me?
I must be dead to you
I know you still wonder
If I'm doing well
I know you meant heaven
When you told me go to hell
I know you still love me
Although you've moved on
We haven't spoken in years
I guess you proved me wrong
You're probably holding on
To what I said to you
How could you forget me?
I must be dead to you

<u>Patience</u>

The guts to appear
When no one else was here
When no one else would hear
The sound of my pain

The nerve of you to stay
When I pushed you away
When I chose to go astray
Your love never changed

The willingness to fight
When I didn't want to fight
When all we did was fight
You took my last name

Regrets

I should've treated you better
You deserve more
More than just words
You've heard it all before
I used plenty of verbs
Seldom any action
Expected you to stay
Without any satisfaction
Expected you to play
I'm so used to women playing
I couldn't recognize
When a woman wasn't playing
You looked me in my eyes
I felt in my chest
You told me you were done
Now I have regrets

Karma

You discovered all the lies,
Every smoking gun,
But your love never changed,
After everything I've done.
You said you weren't surprised.
You knew this day would come.
You gave it your all,
But you knew I wasn't the one.
Once upon a time
Any girl I would shun
Went from grown man status
To acting completely young
I'm ashamed of my actions
The man I've become,
I deserve to be alone
After everything I've done.
I burdened you with my drama.
It must've weighed a ton,
Now I'm waiting on my karma
After everything I've done

<u>Fumbled</u>

I fumbled the best thing
To ever happen to me
I lost her
I wish I could talk to her again
I can't fault her
After everything I did
She tried to forgive me
I didn't make amends
I left her heart broken
Time and time again
I wish I could find her
I lost my best friend
Trying to play field
Now I'm in disbelief
I fumbled the best thing
To ever happen to me

<u>Guilt</u>

All the wrong doings going to catch up to me,
Eventually it will,
That's the way karma works.

The energy you give comes back just as worse,
Negative or positive within this Universe.

God's undefeated and his laws are intact.
Perhaps my good deeds will pull a balancing
act.

We've all fallen short in the courts of God's
judgment.
I hope I'm Forgiven for my sins when I'm
summoned.

Devilish

I've broken many hearts,
Took advantage of souls
Deceived many angels,
With my devilish charm.
I've preyed on the weak,
Entangled the unhappy
I've misled the innocent
I've conquered plenty souls.
I've broken the unbreakable
I've shattered many lives
Destroyed hopes and dreams with my genuine disguise.
I've hid behind a veil,
Camouflaging the truth
I'm a snake inside the grass
I'm a tree with bitter fruit

Hideous

An appetite for destruction
The beast is a savage
That reeks a foul odor
Of spoiled rotten famine
Flesh eating maggots
Hatched from fly eggs
Crawling on my flesh
Bless the living dead.
A life filled with horror
A heart torn to shreds
Sodom and Gomorrah
A city painted red.
Blood for thirst
My cup runneth over
Premeditated sins
From thoughts that are sober.
Hideously handsome
My souls held for ransom
A beautiful disaster
Searching for a sanctum.

<u>The Knife</u>

I've bled on your soul, even though you didn't cut me. A wounded heart needs to heal before it loves.

A dove's innocence with intentions that are pure, you couldn't find a cure for the pain I've endured.

The pressure of love wasn't enough to stop the bleeding. I know you didn't cut me I was already leaking.

Nevertheless, I still bled on your soul, I apologize it was out of my control.

I didn't cut myself, but I tried to do what's right...

Searching for love on the wrong side of the knife.

<u>Undeserving</u>

I don't deserve your love
Your mercy and your grace
I've sinned at will
I've shown a total lack of faith

Despite my shortcomings
Your blessings overflowed
You answered every prayer
Your door was never closed

I still had your favor
Despite my sinful acts
Your love never waivered
You never turned your back

I promised I would change
You never held a grudge
Lord, please forgive me
I don't deserve your love

<u>I wish</u>

I wish I knew then
Everything I know now
A man doesn't understand
Till he's shown how
I wish I had another chance
To take a vow
To make another plan
To cast any doubt
To focus on the Lord
Who I can't live without
Instead of material things
Because they don't count
Broken relationships
That will soon fizzle out
In the end all I have is my soul to think about
I used to dream about
Having more money than I could count
The only faith I had was in bank account
Getting right with the Lord became paramount
When I lost everything, I cared about

Mirrors

My own worst enemy at war with my reflection
I look in the mirror, and I'm ashamed of my image
A bad decision is like a head on collision
I can see it coming but I still can't prevent it
I'm driven by my foolish pride
God is steering the wheel but the devils on the passenger side
In my ear filling it with temptation
It's hard to resist the sensation
I'm easily persuaded
Swimming in an ocean of sin I think I need a boat.
Will I sink to the bottom or remain afloat?
I want to change my ways
But my spirit is broken
When I look in the mirror, I start losing hope

Section 7: Healing

Stars

I'm a star that has fallen
Lord I am calling
Crying out for help
Before I hit the ground
The sound of a star
Explodes when collapsing
Perhaps what I needed
Was to hit rock-bottom
To understand the ceiling
To recognize the problem
Falling to my knees
The only way to call him
Created in his likeness
The image of the Father
Born to shine bright
A start that has fallen

Alive

I wake up every morning and forget to thank
God
Somebody didn't wake up
Somebody's momma cried
Tomorrow isn't promised
Today I could've died
I've taken Him for granted
Yet I'm still alive

Misery

I'm the cause of this feeling
I'm dealing with addiction
I'm hooked on destruction
Accustomed to affliction

Self-sabotaging
Robbing myself of joy
I'm the cause of this feeling
It's something I can't avoid

I can't enjoy life
I'm used to living in misery
Happiness is foreign
Pain's not a mystery

Accustomed to misfortune
Lord, I need healing
No one else to blame
I'm the cause of this feeling

This feeling of dejection
The need to be accepted
Lord, please save me
I need to be protected

Captivity

I've been in captivity
For forty-two years
I've tried and I've tried
To conquer my fears
I've cried and I've cried
I fought through tears
Yet time after time
It fell on deaf ears
Instead of my Father
I turned to my peers
Those whom I loved
The near and the dear
When no one helped
It was abundantly clear
I've never been forsaken
The Lord is still here

Saved

I'm trapped in this never-ending cycle of pain,
I don't want to stop fighting but I'm mentally drained.
My brain is in bondage, my thoughts are in chains,
My hearts behind bars, my emotions are enslaved.
All I've done is suffer; I'm constantly enraged,
My faith is being tested, I don't want to be afraid.
I've fallen to my knees, bowed my head and prayed,
Lord please help me, I need to be saved.

Hero

My mental health is fading.
I think I'm going crazy.
Waiting on God to save me
I've tried to save myself
I could've asked for help
Operating in my ego
Trying to wear a cape
Knowing God is my hero

Faith

A storm is brewing
The calmness is soothing
The wind's picking up
I can hear the leaves moving

As the breeze stiffens
I see the weather shifting
A change in the climate
The sun has stopped shining

The blue skies are fading
The clouds turning cray
The thunder starts to rumble
A downpour of rain

The weatherman predicted
The storm would be passing
His forecast was wrong
It feels everlasting

I see the lightening flashing
Then a power outage
A funnel cloud sighting
Tornado sirens howling
There's no need to fear

Naked

Storms come and go
Trials and tribulations
God is in control.

Father

Although my legs are weary
I run to my Father
This life has me winded
I'm physically exhausted

It's hard to carry on
The grind has me tired
Although I need to rest
I run to my Father

There's pain in my chest
There's shame on my conscience
I'm overwhelmed with stress
There's guilt from my actions

I suffered from fatigue
Relationships are taxing
Although I'm out of breath
I run to my Father

Prayer

Bless me father I'm a sinner
I'm bound by temptation
My flesh has been shackled
I'm a prisoner in hell

Lord, please forgive me
Have mercy on my soul
I'm in need of your grace
Protect me from myself

Be my shield in this battle
My armor and my sword
When the enemy is near
Please wrap me in your arms

Give me sight when I'm blind
Be my eyes in the darkness
When I can't see a way
Help understand your vision

I'm thankful for your mercy
Your love never waives
In the precious name of Jesus
I pray, amen

Warriors

My mother used to pray for me daily, the
praying stopped abruptly, when she passed,
and since then life has been ugly.

It makes me wonder, "Does anybody else love
me?" She can't be the only one who was
praying for me.

Maybe I've gotten some anonymous prayers,
from an unknown source who could sense I
needed God.

Lately I've been waiting for a blessing or
two. So, I need the true warriors to get a
prayer through.

<u>Jesus</u>

I saw a man pushing a cart,
With no destination.
When he noticed me, he stopped
With no hesitation.
He stuck his hand out,
I assumed he was begging,
So, I went in my pocket and offered him a
blessing.
I tried to hand it to him
He said he didn't need it.
I asked him why not?
He said, "All I need is Jesus."

The Cross

There's nothing You can't accomplish.
You can do it all.
No battle You can't win
In fact, You've never lost
No burden is too heavy,
You carried the cross.
Silent words are spoken,
We listen when You talk.
The Holy Spirit's moving,
We exercise faith
Your track record's proven
You never make mistakes.
Anything's possible
I'll never have doubts
The undefeated champ,
You've never lost a bout.
There's nothing you can't accomplish.
You can do it all,
Nothing is too big
No problem You can't solve.
All prayers are answered,
You've never missed a call.
No burden is too heavy
You carried the cross.

<u>The Light</u>

It's dark inside the tunnel
Until I reached the end.
Only then can I understand what the past
meant.
I can see the light, the events that unfolded
Questions that were loaded, unpacked in the
moment.
My eyes wide open, I can see the light.
I know it's not my battle,
I no longer have to fight.
I can give it all to You,
All my worries and my fears,
I may not understand but the Light will appear

Lost you

I nearly lost you
Trying to find me
At war with myself
Searching for inner peace

I nearly lost you
Believing there was more
Only to discover
There's nothing else in store

I nearly lost you
A victim of my trauma
Trying to feel a void
After I lost my momma

I nearly lost you
The only one that cared
When no one else gave
The only one that shared

I nearly lost you
My very best friend
Unconditional love
No matter how I sin

The Greatest

God is the greatest,
I know He has haters,
How can you not believe when there's proof of
His labor?
I've tried Him and succeeded; he answers every
prayer.
I've never been forsaken by my Lord and my
Savior.
He's all I've ever needed even when I couldn't
see it
He wrapped His arms around me during times
of bereavement
No matter what's the season, I know He is the
reason.
God is the greatest, He'll never be a secret

<u>The Burning Bush</u>

I need you, Lord.
I've tried to do it my way.
Nothing has worked,
In fact, I've made it worse.

The bush is on fire
You have my attention
I'll follow your commands
When you speak, I will listen.

My life is in your hands,
You're greater than my problems
There's no need to worry
I know that you can solve them.

The bush is on fire,
My staff is a snake
My shoes are removed
I've exercised my faith

<u>Gracious</u>

I told myself I would do better I did worse.
I said I would pray every day and go to church.
I said I would read my Bible and pay tithes.
I said I would spread the Word and save lives.
Instead of doing everything I promised I would
do,
I focused on myself and forgot about You.
I forgot about the Father, the Spirit, and Son.
I forgot to praise You with every breath in my
lungs.
I forgot to thank You for all the blessings
You've bestowed.
I forgot I have nothing, and everything You
own.
I forgot You can take it, the same way You gave
it.
I forgot about Your mercy, my God You are
gracious.

Divine Intervention

I believed all I needed was her
Until I lost her
Then I realized
All I needed was my Father
The one who's in Heaven
Responsible for blessings
Diving intervention
I'm grateful for His presence
The Holy Spirit moved me
When I paralyzed
When no one else was there
He was right by my side
When one else cared
He listened to my cries
Blinded by grief
He opened my eyes.

Glory

Use this life of mine
Please use it for Your glory
Let my life story a Holy testimony
For those who lack faith
Please point them to my psalms
Use me as an example of how to overcome
Trials and tribulations
Erase any qualms
Provide them with strength
They will need to carry on.
Use this life of mine
Please use it for Your glory
Let my life story a Holy testimony

Rebirth

Lord I'm in a battle
I'm not equipped to win
I need You to defend me
The enemy has strength
I'm not strong enough
Please rescue me from him.
I know I've fallen short
I repent for my sins.
I praise Your Holy name
Through worship and hymns.
Please take me to the water
Although I can't swim
I give my life to Christ
Through thick and through thin
Today I moved forward
A new life begins

Naked

Understanding God

You think you know me well, but you don't
know the half.
You haven't taken the time to learn who I am.
How I failed as a man.
How my plans got disrupted.
How I lost loved ones.
How often I've suffered.
Instead of reading my book, you're focused on
the cover
You don't want to understand you just want to
pass judgement.
You're focused on my luggage, instead of where
I've traveled.
You don't realize all the times I've unraveled.
How my past trauma is a never-ending battle.
Appearing to be strong, but the truth is I'm
fragile.
You think you know me well; all you've gotten
is a sample.
You haven't taken the time to learn what I've
grappled.
But God understands all the pain I've endured
Who I used to be and how much I've matured.
He knows where I've been, where I'm at and
where I'm headed
I'm lost without Him.
He deserves all the all credit.

<u>Rejoice</u>

I can rejoice, even though times are hard
I can rejoice, because my faith is with God
I can rejoice when my pocket is flat broke
I can rejoice, because I'll never lose hope
I can rejoice when my bills are behind
I can rejoice, because I know He will provide
I can rejoice when my health is starting to fade
I can rejoice, because I know He'll make a way.
I can rejoice, despite the pain and affliction
I can rejoice, because of Christ's crucifixion
I can rejoice, although I've struggled with
addiction
I can rejoice, because of Christ's benediction
I can rejoice, while my marriage is in
shambles
I can rejoice, because it's nothing He won't
handle
I can rejoice, through all the moments of
despair
I can rejoice, because it's power in prayer.

Losses

I lost my mom
I lost my dad
I lost my wife
I lost my sons
I lost my daughters
I lost my family
I lost my friends
I lost my job
I lost my funds
I lost my mind
I lost my way
I never lost God

<u>Forgive me</u>

The path I've been walking
The things I've observed
The way that I've been talking
The things that I've heard

The God that I serve
The devil tried to tempt me
The cards I've been dealt
The odds were against me

The emptiness inside
The happiness erased
The false sense of peace
The frown on my face

The places that I've been
The things that I've witnessed
The thoughts that I've pondered
The sins I've committed

The women I've seduced
The ones who believed
The lust that I've felt
The mind that was freed

The dreams that I've had
The goals that I've set
The debts that I've paid
The choices I regret

The mess I've created
The times I was helpless
The child who was lonely
The times I was selfish

The moments I was careless
The hearts that I've opened
The moments I was reckless
The hearts that I've broken

The lies that I've told
The truth that was hidden
The fears I concealed
The cause of my condition

The pain and affliction
The hurt I've held in
The scars from abuse
The wounds from within

The friends that I've lost
The bridges that I burned
The ones that I've crossed
The lessons that I've learned

Naked

The money that I've earned
The self-education
The trauma from the past
The rehabilitation

Naked

<u>Also, By La' Kendrick Thompson</u>

Black in America: The Life and Times of Tank Thompson (Volume 1)

Black in America: The Life and Times of Tank Thompson (Volume 2)

The Truth about Candy

You should have Listened when I told you the 1st time

The Truth about Candy II

9 7 9 8 2 3 4 0 0 5 8 0 9